She Is a Pupa, Soft and White

She Is a Pupa, Soft and White

Poems by Elinor Cramer

Word Press

© 2011 by Elinor Cramer

Published by Word Press
P.O. Box 541106
Cincinnati, OH 45254-1106

ISBN: 9781936370535
LCCN: 2011943591

Poetry Editor: Kevin Walzer
Business Editor: Lori Jareo

Visit us on the web at www.word-press.com

Cover Art: Collection Jewish Historical Museum, Amsterdam.
© Charlotte Salomon Foundation

Acknowledgments

Grateful acknowledgment is made to the following journals in which these poems appeared, sometimes in earlier drafts:

Blueline: "Two Blue-Green Eggs"
The Comstock Review: "Epicenter," "Fish-Pod Weeds in September," "She Is a Pupa, Soft and White"
English Journal: "On a Farm Outing"
The Healing Muse: "Birds, I Said," "How I Waited"
Olive Trees: "Cicadas in August," "Ever," "Now That It Smells of Spring"
Seeding the Snow: "Blossom Eaters"
Stone Canoe: "His Eye," "The Quickening Points," "Chetwynd's Guide"

"During Advent She Can't Eat" received a National Poetry Competition commendation award.

"Hibernation in Turtles While the Faithful Are Waiting" was awarded honorable mention by the Milton Dorfman Poetry prize.

Some of the poems in this book were previously published in a chapbook, *Canal Walls Engineered So Carefully They Still Hold Water*, Valley Press, 2010. Funding for the project was made possible through a Heritage Grant secured by New York State Senator John DeFrancisco with funds from New York State Office of Parks, Recreation, and Historic Preservation, administered by the Cultural Resources Council.

With gratitude to the faculty of Warren Wilson's M.F.A. Program, and to Phil Memmer, teacher and Director, Syracuse YMCA's Downtown Writer's Center. To Barb Kobritz, Jim Ellis, Lori Diekman, Mitch Langbart, and

Catherine Thompson who offered close readings during the preparation of this manuscript, my deepest appreciation. I am much indebted to Jim Flanagan, Steve Reiter, and Kathleen Miles who provided technical support when I needed it, at odd hours and inconvenient times.

Thanks to Kevin Walzer and Lori Jareo for their support of my poems, their skill and their assistance in the process of putting this book together.

Table of Contents

I

Rescue Truck with Its Doors Flung Open............11
Two Blue-Green Eggs................................13
Hibernation in Turtles While the Faithful
    Are Waiting..................................14
Mary's Baby..15
Carp...17
7 P.M..18
On a Farm Outing...................................19
Hominid..20
Forked Runes.......................................22
Blossom Eaters.....................................23
The Gate...24
Warning..26
Once More Again in Love............................27
Estate with Saut de Loup 28
The Quickening Points..............................29

II

The Remains of Mrs. Something Abbott...............33
After the Panama Invasion..........................35
Freedom Plaza......................................36
First in Flight....................................39
Waterproofing the Cellar...........................40
Abandoned Lock.....................................42
The Unmarried Women of Bishop Hill.................44
The House at Congress and Green....................46
Bridge with Sod....................................48

III

Ever..51
Cicadas in August..52
Ringing the Tree...53
Selling My Car 54
How I Waited..55
"Birds," I Said..56
Preparations for the Molt.....................................57
The Crows of Auburn...58
Hoarfrost...59
His Eye..60
Now That It Smells of Spring................................62

IV

Canal Walls Engineered So Carefully
    They Still Hold Water..................................65
Fish-Pod Weeds in September................................67
White Pine: a Metamorphosis................................68
Threshold..69
Chetwynd's Guide..70
Epicenter...71
Midwinter..72
Walking on Snow...73
Creation..74
She Is a Pupa, Soft and White...............................75
Swallows..76
During Advent She Can't Eat................................78

I

Rescue Truck with Its Doors Flung Open

I heard the wranking of diesel engines
and left your book on the chair.
When I pushed back the curtains, I caught smoke
in my throat. There were ladder trucks
and men pulling on rubber coats, slowly,
not to make mistakes that could mean their lives.

A black cloud seemed to envelop the empty house
next door, where Barb lived until last month.
It was still her house to me,
and I tried to call the new number she had written
on a scrap of brown bag—as if to warn her,
a futile arm waving to get out of any harm's way.
But she didn't answer.

Then the firemen disappeared—two houses down,
where TV newsmen shouldered cameras.
It wasn't Barb's house at all.

I went back to my chair and the book you lent,
this after our miserable quarrel.
I let the book comfort me
as though you were reading to me.
But wasn't it my mistake always, to let some object
stand for the one who is gone?
So that I won't feel like the rescue truck
backed into the curb, its doors flung open,
its empty red heart waiting.

When the trucks had gone and no one else came,
I walked around the burned shell.
Wooden drawers of a bureau had splintered on the lawn,
with sweaters, nylon panties, a green plush horse,
its lopsided muzzle chewed and cowlicked.

What you would want to know:
the father drove up to the curb, and sat dazed.
I offered to help salvage.
There, pressed to the car window, a child snuffled
and sucked her collar, her fingers—
all that would fit in her mouth.

With the fingers I used to hold your book,
the stuffed horse she lost—
I began, on my side of the glass,
to trace the child's lips. She pressed them
to the pane till they turned white.
It was a solemn game,
neither of us smiled.
Then I began on her thumb.

Two Blue-Green Eggs

She shows me the translucent eggs
so big they're pushing out of their slots
in the cartons. Two are blue-green.
She has no children, tells me how God
put it in her head to get the ducks.
She turned pages of the homestead journal,
knows by heart: they go back to the Rouen,
the upright Runner, the sky blue egg
of the wild mallard, crossbred by an English woman
named Campbell until the birds are khaki brown.
They are hardy in northern winters,
are meaty and earthbound.

Her mother lost the use of her legs
after a stroke seven summers ago,
sat in the kitchen of this old farmhouse
not even caring to do what her body would still do
until the ducklings were brought home to warm
in a box by the stove. And when their fuzz
was stippled with hollow quills
and they were moved to the fence in the yard,
the old woman asked to have her chair moved outside,
the first time in seven years.

The ducks strut back and forth hardly ever flapping
their wings, too heavy to fly.
The old woman picks her way from the stove
to the table. She would have to remember
the dancing in her legs. The blue-green eggs
have only the color of a light sky over water.

Hibernation in Turtles
While the Faithful Are Waiting

I heard of a man with three land turtles who buries them
in peat moss each fall: Pistol, Fireball and Ulysses.
They move into hibernation, eighteen inches
under the ground. And over them he places lucky charms:
a hood ornament, a blue bottle, a souvenir key chain,
as a father might place a glow-in-the-dark prayer
above the children's bed to watch over their sleeping.

When the other Ulysses returned after twenty years,
it was the faithfulness of the ones who waited
that moved us more than his heroics in war
or his journey home. The old nurse washed
his weary feet before she knew him.
This man washes mud from the stone backs of turtles
and their leather feet in the kitchen sink,
saying, "Welcome home, Fireball. Welcome home, Ulysses."

Penelope becomes even more herself with time.
She turns into constancy the way the turtle draws
its head and feet closer to the heart. The heart suspends
for moments at a time, so that no change is seen.
(The threads are unraveled by night.)
Only the essential lives on. This man sits motionless
at the kitchen table waiting for the turtles' periscope
necks to push through the ground like wedges of crocus.

Mary's Baby

for Mabel

When Mary, my middle sister,
was one hundred and one years old,
I ran the bedpans and changed the linens
along with the aide, the stranger we paid
and trusted in our home. We weren't foolish,
having our eldest sister six months
under the care of a home aide before we lost her.

After a long night of Mary's moaning in her sleep,
I opened the trunk and unwrapped
her porcelain doll. The clear eyes and blush
of lips and cheek gave her, of all our dolls,
the sweetest face that we would know of an infant—
the three of us girls never having married.
Of all our treasures, only the babies with china heads
were shut away—even my broken doll.

I brought her baby to the sickbed.
Mary must have known then, as maybe I did too,
that she was near her end.
She pulled the baby to her chest and she quieted.
In the morning I let her sleep, her arm
still wrapped around her best comfort.
I let the stranger see into our spinsters' heart—
not only the doll, but the pity of it.

The worst next to losing Mary, and after the aide
was long gone—Grandfather's handmade tools
and Seth clock in their places—

was to open the trunk, and find
under the blankets, all of them gone,
even my second best baby.

Carp

Drowsing as at the breast,
lips pumping, then not,
big as that feeder come home.
Only a mouth.

Mud baby, bottom grazer,
sucks root and weed.
He suns near my boat, his chubby dorsal
warming above water
in the shallows.

My boat nuzzles into hummocks
and blackbirds charge from the stubble,
their damp nursery.
The boat and I rock in floating rushes;
water laps at baby's back.

Then the carp's gone—
channeling plumes through the muck.

7 P.M.

In the half-light nothing stirs:
three doves, their puffed breasts
to the damp ground.

The baby stares through me.
Her lips stilled on the nipple,
she moves into sleep.

On a Farm Outing

The only girl I've invited,
Jet suckles the half grown calves: one finger,
two fingers run with their slaver.
More calves nuzzle her wrists and jacket;
they butt and bang each other at the fence to be near
her dripping fingers.

I roll Jet's cuffs and stand behind her.

We watch the farm girl feed the calves from a teat
on the bottom of a pail. They know girls' hands,
their pet, poke and prod. She leads a calf
from the pen with a rope she's threaded through its mouth
and around its snout. It follows after her
with a frisky, colt-like prancing.

Jet-of-the-juicy-fingers wants to be the one
the calves love best. She lives with other half grown girls.
When I visit her, all the girls without
their mothers vie for my attention.
And they soon forget—full of who got more,
who has a pass to go outside.

It's hard to give girls what they want.

None of us pay any mind to the cows.
Separated from their calves
by wire and fence, they lie on their sides, bawling,
their bags and udders engorged.

Hominid

Lucy, you stirred
such joy in those who found you,
they danced to the Beatles song all night;
why do you plumb me
as I look at your bones,
and bring up sadness?

Your remains
are laid rib to vertebra,
humerus to scapula,
in our light,
3 million years after your death.

Looking down on the almost-skeleton,
it's as if I stood
with my first loss,
newly bereft of my mother
and on-my-own.

The ones who named you
chipped for years
to loosen your bones from sandstone.
You're theirs really;
they're fond of you.

They ask, can we know ourselves
from the curve of your ilium,
and how erect you walked.
Then asking of the upward slant of your scapula
where you slept,
might it have been in the trees?

Only five small pieces
of cranium were found,
no bone to suggest
our throats' articulating flaps
and membranes.

Yet, this is the way we place our dead:
arms rest at the sides,
legs outstretched.
Your head, a skull so fragmented
it must have been bashed.

How much better, I think,
had you cradled your brain
with those upturned shoulders,
and hung by your long arms
in the way of apes.

Forked Runes

> *Human beings do not go hand in hand*
> *the whole stretch of the way. There is*
> *a virgin forest in each, a snowfield*
> *where even the print of a bird's feet*
> *is unknown.*
> —V. Woolf, Collected Essays

"Not long," he says to coax me into the cold.
He guides me from the car with his hand gentle,
boxed around mine, to where he looks
over a hillside of chimneys and steeples.

My back is a small animal
trying to raise its hairless muscle
as though that could warm me;
but it can only ache.

I look past our feet into the fresh snow
at the forked runes of small birds
that turn in diminishing circles
before skating away.

Blossom Eaters

Three orioles—my first—dive
into upper branches, and with claws strangling
they bite the pink blossoms.
The sky fumes, never breaking into rain.

From inside the bush comes the sweetest song.
Drowsing on my lawn chair
I'm hearing the song I once heard about rocking
on the tree top, where baby comes to a bad end.
What harsh comfort to sing of her falling.

My neighbor, whose Rose of Sharon the birds invade,
has gone to the lake.
She'll tell me tomorrow that it poured
and they didn't go into the water;
they sat and talked like grownups
behind closed panes. I sit alone in the yard
dimly remembering days lavished on nectar.

The orioles drink and smear
themselves with the juices.
The orange vests bounce as they bend
delicate branches. Oh, we have fallen—
croon it to the little ones.

The Gate

Outside my window, the gate taps
against the post.
It jerks on a short rope and swings back,
bottom taps, but not the top.
Lance and picket partners
wedded together, braced in a Z,
shape each other, their warp and buckle.
They shake-dance in the wind,
pivot on the same hinges,
are in it for the duration.

As a child playing statues,
I was flung down. The little finger
on my left hand broke
where it twisted under me,
and was bound on a splint with gauze and tape
to the next finger to mend.
The broken one grew in a curve
around the knuckle of the stronger.
What an amusing couple, the smaller one
bent to her mate.

I have to remember the half-moons of your fingers
to have them when you're not with me.
When you stroke my wrist it's a homecoming—
never long enough.
The wind rides through the gate
bumping and slamming,
and it tosses the silvery leaves

on the tree outside my window.
They rub against each other
dancing, unbound.

Warning

"The cold snap last night"—
It was cold last night when she fought
with her husband, argued really.
But, this morning with hands in the suds,
her anger wakens.
The TV news is saying—the cold
caught a whole flock of Canada geese.
Locals found them cuffed in ice, their feet bloody
from working at the reddening crust.
She mulls, I should be smarter,
while scouring her retorts
and her cloth around the same cup.

She watches the geese on the screen
hiss and peck at the volunteer's eyes—
how tiring this struggle—
a bird gores his tarsus down to a stump.
"They won't make it," the announcer
says, "if they're trapped
a second night."

Once More Again in Love

> *after a hand colored*
> *woodcut of the Edo period*

At the museum's white wall, the American woman
gazes at the Japanese print:
a woman in kimono fastens a narrow paper,
her face tipped to a flowering branch.
A placard explains, the cheek and blossoms
were hand tinted with the red pigment, beni.
It has softened over the years to pink and yellow hues.
On the small banner, characters of a haiku...

> Once more again in love
> Once more regret—as fleeting
> As cherry blossoms

She wonders at the translation, the oddness
of its twofold affirmation: Once more again...
But she can feel in her muscles
the Japanese woman's body reaching
above her head to fasten the poetic telegram.
Her own arms strain with a tote bag
and a leather strapped purse with bottled water,
her guide books, cigarettes,
and drafts of a letter to her lover;
their pages scribbled and crossed out in a rush
to restate her way of looking at it,
because he wouldn't listen.
Now her feelings begin to change,
this time forming around the words of a verse—
hard, green nubbins.

Estate with Saut de Loup

> *Saut de loup is a deep trench in an
> 18th-century English landscape. It was
> designed to create invisible boundaries
> and the illusion of intimacy with nature.*

The deer have crept from nowhere at dawn
and are poised at the stream below my window.
Their noses aren't to the wind but to the salt lick
and the gamekeeper's feed scattered on the lawn.
The stag's flank is glazed white by the morning sun,
blending it with his pale underbelly.
He looks so close by, it might be possible
to feel moist heat from his nostrils on my breast.
But the sunken walls, the saut de loup, that hold us side
by side, also cut between. At night I am kissed
by another woman's husband behind this closed door.
His heart's chambers flood like mine,
then in a rush are left dry. Tonight he will come.
Tomorrow we will nod and pass among strangers.
The stag stands by the stone trench that lets down
to the reeds. He has grazed by its side many seasons
drinking his fill from my stream.
Now his does and his fawns, their thirst sated,
their muzzles dripping, lift their heads—
and turn on me indifferent tails.

The Quickening Points

He stroked the nose, his hand bristling against the fur,
up to the eye's unblinking stare.
"Is it real?" he asked his mother and the storekeeper,
while he fingered the smooth antler.
The broad male neck curved from the desk top
where the mount balanced. From that sturdiness
it was all taper to delicate nose,
flag ears, and antler, the quickening points.
Restless attention was all in the small boy.
Again he asked as his mother settled the price on the table—
$10 off the 4 chairs, if she'd take those too.
She said it was real, had been real.
Then she was on the phone with his father, asking,
would he help her buy them for her new apartment?
The boy, stirred by her talk of moving,
began to prance about the umbrella stands
and boxes of old picture frames. She found him
in the parking lot with fists full of Queen Anne's lace.
For her, he solemnly tested the dining room chair
he would grow into. Nodding yes to his mother,
the boy slipped back to the mounted head,
ruffed its white under-throat and whispered, "Deerie."

II

The Remains of Mrs. Something Abbott

Archeologists dug beneath layers of dead leaves,
beer cans, and scat, within the wooden frame
of Mr. Abbott's eighteen fifty-something
general store, at Manlius Center,
the canal settlement.
Here are bricks with round edges
they stacked like potatoes and labeled "chimney."

More of their finds are pictured clockwise:
"red transfer-printed whiteware," a fragment
with patterned flowers; and china shards,
"English blue and purple." "Machine cut nail,"
"tobacco pipe stem," and "glass button."
The sign says they were either for sale
at Mr. Abbott's store, or in household use.

Another sign says Calvin Abbott had the help
of his son, James. And a hired clerk.
They lived upstairs. It doesn't mention a wife,

but among the milkweed and grasses at the bank
you can see what looks to be her white roses.
They're low and wild with tiny petals,
and canes re-rooting the path.
They're blooming now. And her yellow iris.
Her name must be like a small glass button
rolled between plank flooring,
not listed with his in a suit for losses
after the canal was raised, and widened.

Yet, if not for her, would Mr. Abbott
have added beveled cupboards?
and an Italianate style staircase.

After the Panama Invasion

after a New York Times Photograph:
January 13, 1990

In an aerial shot over Fort Bragg, the sky is filled
as far as the eye can see
with the translucent tissue of nearly 2000 parachutes,
their dark veins like membranes. Hemispheres ride
the air above a dwarfed transit plane.
Figures suspended in midair reach
their hands over their heads, knees bent.

The wind must batter them as it rushes
into the skins that bear them up.
It must tug at the cords wrapping their chests,
as my heart is borne by the chutes' wafting beauty—
then plummets with the thought of guns
strapped to their chests.
They descend to their wives, husbands and children
cheering below. They float silently

in hordes like the jellyfish, men-of-war,
that invaded the eastern coast of Florida this week.
The great balloons of their bodies, so vulnerable,
rest on top of waves that batter them onto shore,
tear them open. But lifeless tentacles
filled with deadly poison
mine the shallows, rustle in the gentle current
where we tourists in awe of clear sky
wander too near.

Freedom Plaza

> *I went to Washington as every-*
> *body goes there prepared to see*
> *everything done with some furtive*
> *intention...*
> —Walt Whitman, 1888.

Tiring of my conference at the hotel,
the drone of presentations,
I wander outside to a broad median
between arteries of traffic on Pennsylvania Avenue,
and watch boys skateboard on marble pavers.

Under my feet a quote by John Adams
spells the nation's Spirit with a capital S.
Frederick Douglass occupies two squares,
and here is Mr. Ellicott's method of plotting
D.C.'s avenues in the shape of a star
by celestial observation.

Carvings with a flourished script,
as though they flowed from pens,
make me think of the hands, powdered wigs...
their spirits
hover above their names.

A boy's feet smack down;
he staggers across the words,
shaking stringy curls from his eyes.
His yellow board shoots across the plaza
on its own trajectory.
                        That's the fear
I have about our government—it's off course.

Our elders murmur, their words cha-chum
under skateboard wheels.
"...arrayed in glory or covered in shame,"
Douglass says.
                    Without the will
to right itself, I say.

"...we cannot but share its destiny,"
Douglass says.
                    We keep telling them, I say.
I imagine him sighing. Democracy
took years to hear his people.

Now the second president looks perturbed
as a kickflip lands hard
on his blessing of future generations.
I commiserate with him,
words may not last.
                    Not the way the marble
grinds, I say.

The stone re-casts the April sun
with a pearly sheen. And it comforts.
I'll return to the meetings. Soon.
For now the park belongs to us, no rallies,
no police enforcing the skating ban.
Today might be a day like Whitman's reprieve
from skepticism; he couldn't ferret out
any foul motives, he said.
                    Not much happened
during the Cleveland years, I say.

The young man, recovered, scoots his board
in line and cocks it under his toe.
Heat rising off his neck,
he waits his turn.
                    Practice, I say.
I'm betting on you.

First in Flight

She begged to have her long braids cut,
so the boys wouldn't tease her,
the rough ones who liked her, who came up behind
suddenly, catching hold of her pigtails
like reins in their fists. The boys pulled
till she fell with them to the grass.
Then as she scrambled to her feet,
they clucked their tongues
with sounds that meant "giddy-up."

In bed sick most of one day, what a pleasure
it was to lie there, and feel the boys pulling—
as it fastened inside her.
She was reading a book about Orville and Wilbur,
how they built the light craft with their hands.
They were like the boys she knew with paper routes
who waited outside the garage down the block
fiddling with rusty mowers and machine parts,
filled with their secret plans.

Didn't one of them run ahead
pulling the boy on the glider like a kite?
And men were running with ropes tethered
to the small craft's sides. The brother riding
the sateen wings skimmed over ridges blown in the sand,
and she felt the bumping as she read; faster and faster,
his weight bounced on the glider
till it lifted off the ground, and he cried out
to his brother, "I'm flying."
And she felt her whole body
rise from the bed and tremble.

Waterproofing the Cellar

The young men dig with mattocks and shovels
at the fieldstone foundation of this house,
built when slow water carried everything,
when Erie was a canal at the foot of Midler hill,
not the boulevard where two gas stations
and a McDonalds occupy the corners.
And soon, a Salvation Army's rehab
for men and women lost to booze.
Up here, it's the cellar that needs saving,
water's been seeping—washing silt and stones
longer than I've lived here.

You can see how the foundation was laid
from what was at hand: two rows of scabbled limestone
to every one of hewn blocks.
And in the cellar—below the kitchen's double sink
where there had been a wash pump—
they laid a half-walled crypt, a cistern
into which a downspout had funneled rain.
It was meant to be wet on one side, to contain
the flood; but like a living thing, it weeps.

The man whose business it is to tighten cellars,
shoves a chisel between the loosening stones,
showing how mortar crumbled
where rain splashed from the eaves.
The blade buries in the stones' deep pockets.
He shows me chinks between the blocks
big as some I've seen in the aqueduct's walls,
where green algae beards along a spout;
here the stone hosts a powdery mold.

He is older than his workers, a solid man
about my age, closer to the time of old things,
knowing how they worked, and when they didn't,
to the tricks of shim and patch and caulk.

He tells me they'll bleach the mold
and paint the walls with a white waterproof sealer.
White, like the scrubbed limestone you can see
near the Thruway, about the dimensions
of a house's north and south walls—
the remains of a canal lock—dry docked
when bulldozers leveled a swath across the state.
Slab steps on the north from the shorn grass
lead nowhere. There are no wheels, no gears, no gate.

Abandoned Lock

I set out alone
taking the bridge over the railroad yard,
past the carpet warehouse,
where they found the body rolled
from a car into a ditch.

The whine of traffic at my back,
I cross a grassy field narrowed into brush and saplings,
so thick they hide massive gray rocks.

Spooked by a bounding dog,
no, a fawn—
I'm a frozen bull's eye
waiting for the crunch
of a hunter's boots.

I break for the cover of scrub trees,
and climb what looks like block steps
surrounded by heaps of clay
recently left off the shovel,
past Virginia creeper turned blood red,
    and find a trap door—of new 2x4s, set into the stone.
Thick chain threaded through eyebolts.
Padlocked.

I think of the underground bunkers
where that guy on the TV news kept women.

The ones he could catch.

I want to get out of here,
scuttle through the ruins, and mount a wall.
I'm looking into the trough of an old canal lock,
a stream of rippling grass,
with seed heads bowing around my ankles.
The stalks part to show where they're rooted
in the lock's soggy floor,
a long way down.

Imagining myself a measure,
it's as though I'm among them, my feet rooted,
and waving hands over my head,
yet, not the height of their plumes.

I tighten my grip on the slender tree,
but, the grasses have become women
confined in the stones,
their tawny hair blowing,
shush, shush,
sweeping the air.

Then, the plumes change, they're hands
clawing at my ankles,
their wind-muted voices croon:
"You're one with us,
one of us."

The Unmarried Women of Bishop Hill

In a primitive painting,
unvarying women stand in a row
in the morning light.
They look so like each other—
faces eclipsed by bonnets.

The women push long sticks
into the soil, and drop kernels
from pouches at their hips. Slender,
they're like corn stalks
stitched on the rich field.

Beyond the framed scene,
hedgerows of black maple let go,
ravel the boundary
of the church settlement.

Would their sisters, bent to the children,
show distinct faces
within their white brims?
Never the virgins—blinkered
and kept from the eyes
of young men.

In October, they swelter,
lay down their scythes,
and tip their bonnets to funnel the wind.

Seeds spin
from the yellow boughs of maples.

Seed corn,
the yellow hills cry,
multiply, multiply.

The House at Congress and Green

The house in Sandburg's poem
was on the road to three factories.
I read the poem in school,
when I hadn't yet thought of moving anywhere—
certainly not to the city of soot and slaughterhouses.
In the poem the new neighbors hung
white curtains, and horse-drawn wagons
stirred the dust.

Then I moved to the city,
and at night dreamed I carried curtains,
one on each end of a rod,
from bedroom to kitchen window,
never putting them up.

I asked a man I loved
to help me find the house.
I wanted to see, if I could, the house with white curtains,
and imagine what the long ago woman
might say they meant.

Something about hope, I heard the teacher say.
Though it might have been smaller,
a thing women do
when they make a home.

The man drove to every dead-end near Circle Campus,
getting out his map to see
where the streets might intersect.

He stopped the car and we looked over
a six lane expressway.
He said it was probably down there.

It was a time of disillusion,
when people were shooting
at cars from the projects, after King
was killed. My friend wouldn't stop the car
anywhere near the cement high-rises,
where I suppose folks went
when their neighborhood came down.

The woman in the poem washed
and re-hung the curtains,
fighting the dirt,
until she finally took them down.

Bridge with Sod

Daylight is waning. I've been driving for hours
when I come to a bridge, one arch
spanning the lanes.
Capping its brow is a ribbon of grass.
No cars or train.

Maybe it's a trick of light that the scene
seems borrowed from a child's tale.
I expect to see the youngest Billy Goat Gruff
tripping, or the grandfather crossing
to a pasture high in the Alps.

I know I passed under this bridge
a decade ago, before
tall buildings became targets.
Then, I was an unashamed nostalgic.
Looking back wasn't a way of trying
to make sense, as now it seems.

The bridge behind me fades
in the rear-view mirror. I think of the engineer
at his table, sketching a humble margin of turf
to run above a highway,

in the era when our parent's parents
told tales of goats and a girl
under a protective watch.
What story would help today?
Who will wrap their arms
around us, now that we're grown up
and we've seen too much.

III

Ever

One spring swallows whorled in pairs
over the aqueduct and threaded the arches.
I've been back each year,
but never saw them lace again.

Another spring hundreds of swallows teemed
over the roundabout
where boats turned east to west—
birds bowing and greeting on their return.

This spring a flock of kisses brushed my lips,
first the upper lip, then my lower.
With each kiss you led, then waited—
asking me to follow.

Cicadas in August

Cicadas rattle at the screen door
in the choking heat.
They've got summer by the throat
and bring her to her knees.

She falls, the insects fall,
night slides into chill, green walnuts thud
on roofs and footpaths.
Only the slugs cling to walls,

their wet trails rising.
Two cicadas hook like dogs.
No longer fierce against the hemisphere's turn,
they settle for the moment's pure good.

Ringing the Tree

Moths flit around the old trees,
the harrowed elm and hickory's split shingle,
not far above ground—
small wings, pale as bleached leaves
going rapid-fire.

I run home to look for the moths in a book
with colored plates. Rows of insects
are pictured as if held by a pin,
flat with their wings spread open—
unnatural for the moths that can't stay still.

Here's what the book says of cankerworms
and inchworms, spanners and loopers:
Catch the wingless female
with a plaster of molasses, brown sugar,
or fermented fruit when she crawls
from the bark in late fall.

I'm thinking as I read, of the hearts and initials
youth have scratched on the trunk.
And of the male, that incessant flitter,
lovestruck in November,
how he will spread his wings over her and stick
in the sweet stuff—
a final open-mouthed kiss.

Selling My Car

I find him crouched in the ashtray,
a cicada's complete skin among the pennies.
I think *him*, but it's only skin
I finger into a zip-top baggie—
the living bug crawled away
on a spare set of legs.

When he comes from my pocket,
comma legs are stuck in the plastic's margin;
his casing's crushed like bits
of a beer bottle—light playing through.

He's the stain of tobacco juice,
an old man's spit,
the glow of tarry medicine
in a stoppered vial,

a jewel come from within,
cousin to tortoise shell
and goat's horn crescents
worn on the wrist.

Amber lantern, honey pot, and my copper cents—
I say what he reminds me of
as I drive off.
Then I toss the cicada's double,
broken, no longer a likeness,
to the grass and the ants.

How I Waited

after Milton

When I couldn't see the umbels
jutting their parasols among the weeds,
or the long grasses stitched
in the direction of the wind's sweep,
and when the clouds on both eyes were
thick as the sky bursting in showers,
I railed at the candelabra spikes,
the tipping stalks and spires,
and upbraided the fading light,
the trees for tossing and bowing like
waiters serving a feast,
not meant for me—
and the impossibly small birds
that flitted in the branches.

"Birds," I Said

My vision with implanted lenses
lets me see the sparrows—
they don't vanish as they once did,
too far and too small to see.

And brickwork now
sports angles sharp as those we drafted
in geometry class.

If I've ever seen with such clarity,
it's been that many years—
since I was in school.

One, and two birds fly
into a crack staggered down
the bell tower.

They perch and disappear
into the facade,
with what, sticks in their beaks?

I grab the binoculars
I bought before the surgery—
when the doctor told me
to order, and he would deliver,
what it was I wished to see—

the stars in the sky,
or the needle's eye.

Preparations for the Molt

When the heat goes, as we knew it would,
I enter the chickens' steamy enclosure
from the sweeping draft of the yard.
I unlatch the small door
and round my shoulders,
making myself over
to the dimensions of their world.

Dust stirred by bruising wings
settles dry on my tongue;
webs of summer-dried flies catch
on my hair and eyelids.
Soon it will be dark. My beady eyes blink.
The boldest stretches crumpled claw,
jutting her neck to peck at snow
clinging to my survival boots.

I buckle my legs and make home
in their basket. The birds roost
on my knees, huddling against the chill
that creeps through the boards.
Heat radiating from their cloacae
drops wet on my apron.
When I shift in my sleep, they rustle
and moan their blind cautions.

The Crows of Auburn

> *The city's wintertime roost,*
> *estimated at 65,000 crows...*
> —The Post-Standard

The guys at Curley's bar
have had it up to here with splats
covering their cars after happy hour.
They congregate near bright mirrored bottles,
while crows commute in the dwindling light
to trees that rim the bar's gravel lot.

Some say it's the lamps flooding the yard all night,
and the river outlet nearby.
What is it with the men—some wearing ties
and others in jeans stiff with mud, layered
over thermals, wind-reddened cheeks—
that gets them talking of guns?

State law, you can't smoke in a bar;
they move to the lot and slap
their arms in the cold. Men who wear side-arms
for their jobs talk of shooting with men
who talk sport—turkey and deer.
Together they talk crow.

Hoarfrost

Tonight the moon is hanging
between the maple's black limbs,
crooked as a Cheshire grin,
and fading, the way light fades
through a narrow slit.

It's so cold,
the big, yellow cat I feed scraps
banged the plastic bowl
against the porch, licking
the crust of grease.
When I opened the screen
a circle of light spilled on his ear,
the way it's been since summer
scabbed over with blood and tar.
He won't let anyone put a hand to him.
Then a rustling behind him,
and the naked tail of a 'possum
slithered down the stair.

The two of them together—
crazy as moths that bang
their wings at my lighted kitchen window.
The moths have lost the yellow moon and mate
with the yellow window pane instead. Why not?
Tonight frost eats their silvery wings.
I'm in a threesome
with the dish and the spoon.

His Eye

Mahalia was singing in my head,
"His eye is on the sparrow…"
when I got out of bed to pee.

The October moon,
making brilliant squares
of the window shades,
is everywhere—

And now my father's riddle
from long ago
chases out her contralto:

"I rode my bicycle to market today,
and Yet I walked."

Each guess I made
what a child could make,
"Oh, Daddy, you don't ride," and,
"You can't do both at the same time."

The five year old that I was, conserving
what I knew of logic.
But it was easy when he explained
it as language:
a dog named Yet I.

Tonight's simultaneity—

the moon in every window,
not first the kitchen

then the study—
defies all notions.

Which must be why
Mahalia sings it the way she sings it—
so you know it's a big deal:
at once,
all the sparrows.

Now That It Smells of Spring

a white dove flutters at the round window
of Second Olivet
trying to hump a gray pigeon.
But the ledge is barely deep enough for one.
She doesn't budge.

Bright afternoons give way to cold nights.
The pigeons return to winter flocks,
huddling stiff in their rows.
I reach blindly in the drawer for socks.

In the morning I watch two pigeons chase
along the roof and steeple;
the pearl gray hovers mid-flight
letting the white dove flap
along her back—ta da,
a muffled clapping with gloves.

IV

Canal Walls Engineered So Carefully They Still Hold Water

We didn't know you'd be leaving
when we chose the old canal in June,
brought a picnic in a splint hamper,
and walked the towpath to the aqueduct.
It still carries water, reduced to a sluiceway
where it was mended.
Capstones had toppled into the canal bed
like grave markers.
That's when you told me that a man we know,
out of kindness, mowed
between the carved headstones
abandoned outside his village,
no descendents to remember.
Now he too is gone.

You read to me from your father's letter,
how he dressed your stepmother,
complained of her putting slacks
over nighties and slips, and her juice
forgotten before the glass was drained.
Moving to Minneapolis you might shore up their lives,
you said; and I understood
your husband was less needing of you, your lives
already changing.

We ate our lunch and talked about your daughter,
my poetry—the way people speak
when they want to leave something to remember.
I focused my eyes on a few square inches of limestone—
miniscule spider-crabs trapped in the secretions

of early ocean cells—
wanting to read in the fossils
how each trembling day was lived, unaware
it might be the last.

You write and tell me she doesn't remember you,
who show her photographs from old albums,
her grammar school graduation, her first husband
in an Al Capone hat.
Cool water trickles through a gap in the aqueduct,
box elder and rue breaking through the mortar.
The woman who wears chiffon in the photos
clicks her tongue and slowly,
as if memory were borne a drop at a time,
names the guests at her wedding.

Fish-Pod Weeds in September

Along the canal, milkweeds with broad leaves
fatten the pods familiar to my childhood,
the ones I used to split mid-belly
to find a fish with pearly scales,
plump and slippery in a milky sea.
Once I ran home with one, sticky in my hand.
But Mother said it couldn't be a fish,
not if it grew in a field. She put a clothes pin
in her mouth and snapped a wet towel to hang
before she peered into my cupped hands.

Surrounded by asters spreading their purple rays,
the milkweeds of the canal seem to say,
you are young again, and Mother
swims in our field.
But when I open a pod, the scales are turned
to brown seeds, and have begun to separate,
each on its own silk strand.

White Pine: a Metamorphosis

Bark broken into troughs and ridges—
as if veins wove the bare trunk—
runs shallower to her nipples, ringed
and wizened. Twisted sticks
shoot two at a time from small mounds.

Her limbs are all elbow and wrist
swollen at each joint,
and have been bare, easily,
as long as I've been alive.

Far above, new branches billow like sleeves
by the hundreds; her green bodice
shakes and rustles in the breeze
like a costume she wore when a girl.

(That was long ago, when she ran from him.)
Now it doesn't cover.
I can see from where I stand, under her dress,
the arms and legs of a once spindly girl,
gone gaunt and spinster.

Threshold

All summer I've been reading Emily Dickinson,
cloistered in my yard by the stockade fence.
Wasps tap against the pickets;
when I turn, they hover at the sweet wood.

The yellow and black insects
are my closest company, their gentle drone around
and between the sounds my throat makes
for words written one hundred fifty years ago.
The wasps bump at this threshold,
muddling impressions,
                    insistent as souls
bumping their heads their first try out of the body.
I think they're ones Emily attended,
preparing them for their eternal beds.
Or Susan, gone after her, slipping notes
to Emily through my fence.
They're not done with her—
and now that we're gathered in my yard,
I don't want my time with her to end.

Yet, evening's coming and I'm hungry.
She turns back at the stair.
Distinctions—no longer blurred—my stomach,
my voice saying toasted bread.

The wasps slow in the cool air
of a summer almost over.
They crawl into the turned sod,
bury themselves in the earth.

Chetwynd's Guide

When you dream of catching a train
that plunges through the night
toward some destination
you never reach, how would you know
after these many years—
until reading Chetwynd's dream book—
it's your longing for the dead?
He warns against trains,
their trajectory of grief.
If only you had dreamed of a small house,
he says, with a red door
between mullioned windows—
your mother's face.
You wouldn't have fussed half the day,
kitchen to bath to the bookshelf,
chasing after the silver coach
shunted from its wheels,
and lowered into the ground.

Epicenter

I woke to Henry, my boy-cat this morning,
though he's been dead six years.
He used to stretch across my chest, his weight so light,
it wasn't he who disturbed my sleep.
But I'd wake to his warmth when winds beat
maple branches against my porch.
Once the bed swayed to gentle tremors
of a quake rattling the wardrobe doors
in their frame, chattering a saucer and cup.
Henry, his eyes wild, his crying, a high shriek,
accused the bed, the rattling doors
and me of changing.

Last night he came as if called
by the shifting epicenter of another grief.
He came from under the rhubarb leaves,
stepped on the loam where I had dug
through crusted snow to bury him at the twisted grape.
I reached my hand to where I saw him, small and gray,
my hand not yet touching—
And in my outstretched arm, plain longing
shifted some tectonic plate,
heaving me from sleep.

Midwinter

Was it only last Tuesday I fed the hens
on a harsh morning, and found the first egg
since the waning days of summer?
Beside the egg was the old bird, its neck

a broken question, frozen under the roost.
What could have moved her in the blind night
to lose her hold on the bough?
Now the maple sloughs off snow,

but its whiteness is deceptive,
its drip-drops bleeding.
While fingers rooted in my swollen body,
every tissue said, 'yes,'

to the beginnings of a child. Then I went stiff
thinking, "I won't be able to care for you."
Like snow from the roof,
you fell away, blanket, cradle and all.

Walking on Snow

I strap on snowshoes and trail
last year's weed heads
poking through snow.
A goldenrod stalk swells
over a spotted fly's larva—
all that protects it
from the shriveling cold.

Then I set out across the lake
swinging one heavy foot
ahead of the next—
I'm learning to walk again,
entrusting my skin
to a fragile crust.

Creation

Snow swoops along a driveway and drafts upward—
I expect to see someone at the garage door
almost hidden by drifts.
But it's the wind. Having banked into this canyon,
it eddies and whips yesterday's snow
into a glintering storm. There is no snow blower
thrusting a steady spray, no mechanization,

yet it resembles the cascades,
back-lit by a moon that arched over the ski slopes.
There was a family of Salvadorans with me
who had not seen snow until these weeks.
So we drove into the empty parking field—
with the hiss and drone of equipment
filling the chill air—as if we
were the only ones alive to witness creation.
Then a jeep emerged grinding from the snow shower
and slowly climbed the hill.

I spoke in English, a few words, to say the machines
were making snow and the ones with me nodded
with solemn faces, seeming to consider this
against whatever their lives had held
of the momentous or of human folly.

Then the sky whitened around us and I turned
on the headlights and drove into a storm.
And as the windshield glazed over with flakes,
their child bounced on her seat, chanting,
Nieve. Nieve.

She Is a Pupa, Soft and White

She is white, legs immobile,
tapering on the sheets,
her white gown pulled
above the soft masses of her thighs,
head shaven, small and white
on the pillow.

She is a pupa, soft and white,
curled at the heel where the muscles
won't work that side
of the body. That hand, curled,
rests on a sheet to keep the fingernails
from digging into her belly.
Only her voice says
catch-me-if-you-can, like the time
before her sickness
when she disappeared for days
and we found her in the soup lines
at St. Michael's.

The nurse asks me to help smooth
the sheets under her, and as we turn
her toward me, a butterfly
tattoo needled in blue
above a blue moon, appears to rise
from her gown's folds
and to crest, wings open
on the horizon of her thigh.

Swallows

Swallows dip suddenly from a cloudless sky,
wheel along the stream
and under the aqueduct to nests
stacked like pueblos in the arch,
and their babies' beaks outstretched.

Their plummet mocks the heart's drop
to the stomach in fear.
They're like Mexican divers who plunge
from the highest cliffs to the reefs
for pennies—but more than the pennies,
it's the grace of falling-free.

Because the swallows mount and drop
and slide through again,
it must be letting go that they've mastered,
like the crows whose laughter echoes
across the Kremlin squares.
They slide down the gilded cupolas,
their wings and will tucked to their sides.

This is how we practice our deaths:
throw ourselves headlong,
eyes open, without prayer.
Our blouses billow,
as when we were tossed in the air as children,
before we knew we would be caught.
But before it was too late,
we were caught.

What we desire is the body suspended,
long enough, between what is
and what—in one more second—
could be.

During Advent She Can't Eat

For three weeks she has sipped nothing but water,
the smell of broth makes her sick.
Afraid I will hurt the hard lumps
under her arm, she pulls against the mattress
working her legs slow, like a kick under water,
but cannot turn her heavy body.
When a cramp stiffens her leg,
I massage the wasted muscle, but the pain
is trapped in the loose garment of her skin.

Each day she fingers open a paper shutter
on the Advent calendar, made three dimensional
into a house with gabled roof. Behind the apertures
are pictures for the days until Christmas,
so that time moves through the house
from the garret to the front door.
Through the windows she shows me a poinsettia
on a table, a maid shaking a feather pillow,
two cats, orange and black spotted,
like the two that crouch near her bed.
There is one double-arched door
unopened this Christmas Eve.

I light a candle beneath the paper house—
Yellow glows through the paper windows
illuminating the slow days of Christ's coming.
Breathing shakes her chest, escapes
through the open slit of her mouth. She sleeps
and dreams she wraps a long scarf around and
around her neck, turns the knob,
and steps across the threshold on new snow.

Elinor Cramer is the author of a chapbook, *Canal Walls Engineered So Carefully They Still Hold Water* (Valley Press, 2010). Her poems have appeared in *Stone Canoe, The Comstock Review, English Journal* and elsewhere. She holds a Master of Arts degree in psychology from Roosevelt University in Chicago, and an M.F.A. in creative writing from Warren Wilson College. She lives and practices psychotherapy in Syracuse, New York.